At the Point of Seeing

At the
Point
of Seeing

MEGAN
KITCHING

OTAGO UNIVERSITY PRESS
Te Whare Tā o Te Wānanga o Ōtākou

CONTENTS

Blue-tide

With half an eyelid
I step over the eggshell night
unwoken.

Out of indigo pools
trees and houses
yawn, unlace their black coats.

When Water Was a Galaxy

In the Wintergarden, what joy
totting up mandarin fish
with my tantalised fingers

kneeling to tip the bowl
of an inverted world where water
boatmen skimming over silk

opaquely jade and lily pads
were mere opening acts
for those twists of amber flame.

Grazing grottoes, sliding in
and out of watery doors
only their fins could conjure

or placid with mouths agog
they'd hang in the gulp
between want and reach

— then vanish
as a handkerchief whisked aside.

The Horses

The horses in the paddock out front were dead
but I didn't know watching their sway backs
like any pony-mad girl up the drive and into
the house narrow smoky-green walls a tartan
of brasses trophies frames I couldn't put my
finger on what was so gentleman's hunting
lodge its canine reek and portraits of greyhounds
they raised and raced the women who ran
the farm and as soon as I'd seen the dogs
in newspapers rosettes and rug hair there
were dozens among us slipping swift over
the grass out the back away from the ponies
to the barn where the women worked together
alone on their land in a way I didn't quite get
unless they were sisters then through the door
a hunk of macrocarpa like a horse's panting
chest stained ribs out of their cage propped
on the block huge bloodied bone for her
axe to split with her stocky shoulders
in a quilted vest and the hounds at her heel.

Memorial Museum

There was not a drop of water
in the gallery of shells.
Just vaulted, marmoreal air,
a deadalive alpine light
over cabinets,
meaning little cabins,
confiding to my tiptoe lean.

Beside the shells' untouchable
tea bowl beauty, their aural porcelain
curves, sat a knowledge
clear-cut as glass, covetous
and arcane: each echoing name.

Though the gallery is gone
my awe remains at the fathomless
work of the array, the way
it offered a certain world.

Each in its niche, tucked,
all in place yet all depending
on the specimens, case by case,
washed up or plundered, prised
apart from their lives,
then husked into drawers you could slide
to hoist the streaming seas
for inspection.

There they lay, whorled pools
in gaping sockets, strange
to the leached colours of air.
The architecture of armour
and display filling halls
columnar and close

with the mysterious whisper
of alabaster and paper.

Botanising

I'm sitting on the gravel where the cars pull in
outside the paddock gate. It's too early for devices
so as my pony grazes I dawdle my hand among the weeds.

Knowing the pleat of a plantain leaf, I tug and knot
the hairy stem around itself to spring the feathered nub.
It jumps a distance and I look after, idly.

There I discover a thing: that this verge of afternoon dilates
the closer down I get. The grain and scatter makes me small
of quiet. There's a drift here I can follow.

Into the corolla of a flower. Say, a buttercup:
its name is to lightly hold, to settle on this yellow brim
that cradles me as I sit there still.

I still remember sitting by the road's edge
in the petals when a ute's tyres crunched and a man
leaned out to ask me what I was doing.

With no thought I said, I'm waiting to be picked up.
If you stay there you will be, he told me. But I am distinct
from that flower and from him, as I had noticed.

Weeds

1. Pūhā
(*Sonchus kirkii*)

Growing with abandon in blue-grey swathes of before
on these coasts, heads in the clouds, he ao, he aotea

while on seas dark-dyed with trade men mark up
where the world begins and each thing circumscribed within.

      It grows and we pick, we rub and we cook, we eat
      and laugh and shit and it grows and we pick. We don't need

      your books and your lists. Wouldn't you rather hear
      what common-or-garden gossip's brewing?

All the same it's drawn out of the ground into the salts and soot of ink
the supple remembrance of the page, the pose, that bristly jizz

which the tangata whenua know: tender, stringy greens with mussels
hot stone steamed even before the ships sail in with their pigs.

      Sow thistle gets under our boots, we diggers
      of slip and gully seeding fast as we can clear. How like home

      the native can look. But a weed's a weed and we can leave
      chaps like Kirk to sort one from the other.

Now the endemic strand clings to capes and cliffs
      where scientists stoop to record and it's the Pākehā
pūhā we spray or eat for old times' sake, a bitter reminder.

11. Goosegrass
(*Galium aparine*)

shoulder-tap you're it
wimp sticky weed
splat down your back
haha got you green
graffitied T-shirt tailed
with dribble stain of can't
throw can't catch
didn't make the team

run & laugh   laugh & run
those daydreams
of the field whip by
in white-starred lime
my arms flung high
smash the line   yah
I'm the fastest in my mind

OK also-ran is not
so slack
it's how you roll
sprawling unsung corners
see a patch it's game on
& you with your easy
pull-tab strings
suck up & play along
no feeble eye for a hook
you spot a kid & go
all clingy
even now
this grown-up racing
so smart looks
behind finds she
has green all over

III. Herb Robert sonnet
(*Geranium robertianum*)

He capers into the shade your back casts
the moment it's turned. Likely corners fern and
froth, rosette on rosette outspreading fast,
gossipy as a teahouse tablecloth.

His puckish, Robin Hood dance, all floss
and rhubarb pink, makes ditches cackle. Spells
tucked in his motley passementerie; lost
along with the roadside tales he could tell.

Long overgrown, shoved in the back drawer now
with crockery and twee. Those ancient names
too folksy to fly: doves' feet, cranesbills, crows.
Garden-gate love gone rank with blood and game.

But look, his electric kinking seed-beaks,
the way they chuckle, the pidgin they speak.

IV.

(*Hedera helix*)

Albertus Magnus wondered if the joining of ivy
and tree united two souls.
For such lapping you want
the elementary spirit, a tepid stem-pulse
watery and light and strung with sun.

It was roped to the hedge.
I had to hack to uncleave
its evergreen, hand over hand
hauling through stalwart lonicera.
As a house goes down, as a ruin, as a long
demolished wall whose burgeoning
got in the way of arcadia.

So I tore them apart, dug and sucking
root. Leaving my bare arms snarled
with the prints of its climb
still stinging. Those miming
filigreed fingers clutched
a sudden sky. Overborne,
loop and hasp undone.

The hedge lay broken across the lawn
and ivy hawsers
cut, dried, lit, rushed their ashy lips
over chimney brick: last kiss.

v. Rimurapa / Bull kelp
(*Durvillaea antarctica*)

what if you dream you're an oil rig
what if a surge slips your coils
    and holdfasts fail
what if you're sure the spectrum tastes toxic these days
what if you're right
what if you're suspended in nutrients lit from above and all this
    is no more
            than nerve-pictures sifting down screens
what if you fall in love with your own cyanotype
what if your smashed raft survives the circling
    you establish a colony   it's going well
what if you're self-lubricating
what if viscously dreaming in strange motion you discover how
    to swarm
what if you arrange yourselves into avenues, parks and monumental
    radial groves
what if rumour arrives of trees with dreads like someone you knew
what if you can't bear to imagine rimu
        weeping for centuries buried in air
what if you worry about fluctuations until you gnaw through
what if you just unplug
what if against all medical wisdom you still get ice-cream headaches
what if you learn that ice-cream is the harvest
    of your brown relations whose alginates
        can slow the melting

Houseplants

The fern fronds its dinky table, epiphyllum sprawls in a chair
pulled up to the window. The aspidistra has the floor.
The plants of this lounge are sturdy with abiding; they sit
astride the banal hours and feed like mussels on any
light that washes in. When you come home some are waxen,
tight-lipped, admonitory. Others are curved, coy, uplifted in a wave
yet unmoved: your whatever mood like your talk merely
brushes past, a puzzling draught. The plants have engaged
this room for a long smoke of a dusty thought. You catch
the murmur of their wry, cross-stemmed turning round the pot.
Stymied at times, stunted at the tongue for missing the water
you dole out but tending to love whenever sun sidles over.
How it mottles leaves to blush, raises their pitch of bristling
stillness until time drips from their epidermis sweet as liquorice.

The Bending Moment

The pocket fractometer
is brass-black, a serious
thing to gravitate the palm.
It comes in a leather pouch
like a ransom. Imagine
the instrument weighing
the heart as it tests wood:
curving a core drawn from
the fissured, fungal whole.
The fractometer finds the bending
moment of a tree. It sounds
decay, leans a load upon
the hollow parts to see
if bole like bone will bend
to what angle of strength.
Because lignin bears.

The pocket refractometer
is digital-white, eager
as a dowsing rod. It plays
with the high jinks as light hits
liquid and bends in new
directions, surprising no one
who raises its prism
or looks into its well.
The meter reads concentrations
by tiny forks. The way
incidents angle in
through various tears.
When we are reduced
to ferment, airborne sun
falling on surface tension,
it confirms our dissolution
into salts, sucrose, sap.

The value of refraction
also holds for blood
which will return to rain.
Because water clears.

Crematorium

What a word. So Victorian. Hygienic in the mouth.
      Open it like a nut, a decorous crack of the throat,
a hushed aspiration. Syllables roll like an asphalt road through
     the rounded o to the i,
           come to rest at the end, the em, the um.

Vowels buttoned down on a plush lawn. A lone
    cross against a bright blank sky.

Verona by the Leith

By laying a rope to stage the grass
    in a garden in a park
and lasso the sun to slow
    the hours: these two, presently

By shaking out a tartan rug, by opening
    pottles, bags, saying hi
(shuffle and revolve like cats,
    settle down you lot)

By intoning a conch
    to cast us, subdue the sky-light
and stave off the cold front:
    here's the prologue blowing in

thumping bass of kererū
    and backchat, the old russet
touch-paper swagger, thumbs
    up we get that (someone's dog yaps)

By playing it fast, tribal and green
    in street clothes they're a motley
among and apart, mingling with kahikatea's
    tombstone pillars

and the kids fidget and adults drink,
    the day dissolves into trees
and centuries of evening
    come over us and again

By speech lying in ambush
    and the blood blush and the sap
and resurrecting the joke
    and by the word *vial* you just know

By the weeds, roots and leaves
  right underneath as close as sleep,
a gull's cry slicing not the saddest act
  but some ordinary line.

And With Us in Chorus

here's summer's cicerone
>   revving up his seven-year resurrection solo in the stems
his thimble of glass-green
>   armour hardening to macho snare drum staccato
for she for she who'll gather
>   him and shimmy through their hot afternoons of electric mesh
wings unzipping in the blue
>   roar peeling off these poplar-tousled days
under sun's signal power
>   wishing on the dandelion rotary clothesline clock
for love among the cryptic
>   cicadas who cycle into haiku text tone syllable sips
their rice-rattle sweeping
>   a thousand zones of somnolence

Cold Fusion

Loping out each morning, board-beaked,
flashing arms breaching the foam, they paddle

into their elastic time zone where they swirl
and lull like birds riding thermals.

Lilted, cycled, nudged back a wave's length
to hang, pyramidical buddhas

with a point in view, the sea washing
under their ribs and legs, its neoprene burn

and that rolling roar in their ears, cold
fusion of surge and horizon. Till a decision pending

in the swell brings the board's nose around,
sped edge bubbling up to quick sprung

drop into that slipping, joy-long upright
chase along the wave's dynamo purr all too soon

spent. So they turn, prone but restless,
thumbed over and over, erased by whitewater

merging with the breaking lines
unborn before they surface and reform.

Mornington

A morning rain of muslin, hardly there
except in the pinprick flicker, a thickening
of the air. Far then farther the cars down
watery tunnels shrink while every branch
and blade swells into closer green. The leaves,
poised, tuck the mist between crease and rib,
now and then bouncing to shed a drop
with a quiver. In such twitches and glints the rain
gathers, finds runnels and nubs in concrete
that coil clear water into guttered dark.
What remains, drifts: the road a stippled mirror
of a hushed and hooded suburb whose colours
through wet hours deepen, become more patient.

A Bee Against a Window

A bee against a window
crawls, sidles, then drops
dogged, like a swimmer
under a waterfall pummelled
by the pipe-organ drone
of its own labours. The glass
viscous as summer air
ripples with grains of light.
Flowers stain those waves
and the bee quivers, tasting
(not quite yet) their sweet sonar,
shoulders steadily on.
The blunt head nudging
for a change of pressure,
a crack where its song
will mute, a swallowed echo,
and rush through into streams
beyond. The bee knows no sides
only sunwards until
it tires, rests in the hammock
of a corner. It cannot lie
like glass or twist colours
like distance or sly through
that other, open window.
But climbs steadily on.
One instant lofted free
and the bee will forget
with what patience it now
gnaws towards a day
upon the rim of summer.
Between is this wing, this waxen
slice of sky, this slipping wall
the bee scales, forever.

Hiatus

Sun, silence. As if a great gong
had rung overnight. Streets remain
edged in pencil: a brown-blown
rose, fences, speechless windows.
Cut-out shadows of parked cars
lean into an absent wind.

A plane hangs, no closer to land.
From the beach the hush of surf
then the heavy startling passage
of a voided bus. In semaphore
someone has signed their lawn
in cabbage tree leaves.

Asymptote

He's there after all, a lone bowler,
before the grey bloom has dried
from the green, morning's gate
breached with no fuss, his bag
plump on the clubhouse step.

Where his trawled tracks end,
bruised arcs of footfalls across
that dew-frosted field, he stands
like a man whose just-ex wife
has left him holding the phone.

Its clunky Bakelite has gone dead
leaving him decades to figure
out what to do with the black
pendulum that hangs uncradled
from his hand, disconnected.

While in sight near the shuttered
building a quincunx of bowls
mulls over their bias, the curve born
in them like a voice aches along
a line, brushes it without quite

Retracing

Two people stroll where the sand will hold them,
the middle band of dusk which remembers enough sea
that they can walk half on water. Imagine this so
so ordinary couple passing
                              a slick of kelp
thick skin turned   bone blazed with a
yolk-orange lip
                     and nothing said, easy in
each other's hours. The pattern of their insteps
wavering over and along their beach
                          as seagulls shuttle
like forklifts   back and forth
blinking red feet.
                     Imagine just
then she stops, stoops and
          her hand   is shell
          creamy light beams up
          thumb curves whorl
          it is a wonder
                     her husband ahead now
behind his back
          her blue paisley
          dress drapes her
          hair and her downcast
          look fully inside
          her find.
                     On he walks,
his salt-grey head keeping company with
the crunch of steps he takes for hers. Here
linger half with her catch of breath and with
the other wait for his falter, his halt
which comes so late his pace is fraying its
edges and ponder how far his sight is set
into wind or stubborn distance when at once he

                             hears, listens,

turns.
           Now imagine how taken
           aback he is by a stranger
           where he left his wife
                  lost so gone an ocean's
           moment

just before
             he casts his mind along
             the waves' white lapping
             wander to her feet.
             Picture her standing, still
a girl's intent in her
               gleaming voice
                   look
                       look
                           what touches me.
Imagine him retracing   taking   her hand.

On Hume's Table

I was writing on Mr. Hume's table.
— ROUSSEAU

David Hume is thinking, 'This very table.'
This table here, can't you perceive how very
it is? How square in its four-footed proof
of things, how they bed in existence,
this table, 'which we see white,
and which we feel hard'. I like

to peer through the words at him,
this philosopher, whom we see white,
prodding a finger just to check.
'The paper, on which I write at present,'
his pen scratches, 'is beyond my hand.'
And whoomph: time's very
edifice collapses
none of it has happened
and some atoms we breathe
are back in the body
of a man who sits
at a window, presently
casting his eye like an angler's hook
over the 'great extent of fields and buildings'
the chamber, the walls,
his cramped hand
drawing the ink
across the paper
on the table.

Doodler

I knew a man whose blue-black art
                        ran rings around any speaker.
Whatever the talk, his brambling
                        curlicues would clamber over.
The pen rocking the skull's cradle
                        let the lizard brain out
on its agile feet, eyes of jet
                        ink hooking this to that.
We'd watch the nib work
                        the page into indigo lace
until our pupils spiralled
                        like dazed-eyed cartoons
dancing on a paper shoreline
                        lapped by a tattooed sea.

Watch Out Walkers

Ms Walker is a caution. How she lost
her tell-tale feet she can't stop to say

not even to me, her pedestrian fellow.
She is round the bend, a tragic figure

hung on a pole. Truncated by her panic
she spurns the ground, elbows swinging,

all aslant as if she's flying from a lurker
in the park. Ever since a truck

or speeding van snipped off her hands
she has suffered a bitumen tongue.

She can only sign in loudest neon:
Walkers! Watch out for yourselves.

Arabica

go on, refill
your hands
in deference

or deferral
of else-hood
cupping

momentarily
its small
transport

through froth
to burr
and bitter

ground
between
have and not

as in
what's left
of our manu-

factories
the young
burn oil

to sell
rich blood
new brinks

Appropriation

Start from this: someone once saw an elephant.
At least one anonymous elephant was seen, heading west:
the bracket of the ear, bucket legs, the trunk's clinching
hook. Over the beast, a howdah holding sway, a suggestion
of plumes conveying the unattainable rider. That's pattern,

now copy. Out of a woodblock translate that parade
of trumpeting thunder to a stamp. Body to ground, ground to
body, each impression reducing elephant to bloated
lozenge, trotting corgi. Until it's all but emoji.

Multiples of elephant woven back and forth
in every position but origin. Slapped on a cushion
stacked in a would-be continental boutique
on a street named for some governor
and thrown across this sofa
wincing their Babar smiles.

Cover made
in China.

Cover: 100% polypropylene.
Fill: Polyester fibre.

Armrest

In the rest home: the rest. Down this one-way street
you meet the commune's terrarium gaze.

When you pass you relent under that wait without
knowing why. Those chairs and faded frames, coiffed heads
and chairs with arms, arms on all the chairs.

In the hospital: the patient. You, filed within glass
turning amber, mulled over by muted doors.

On seats with scratched adjustable legs you fill out
your frail understanding, soon,
of an arm bracing a hand,
a hand holding an arm that rests on a chair.

The Artist's Site

Behind the screen a woman is walking
rubbing her hand-sight along the grain
of a monochrome land. As far as paper
scrolls she draws its jawbone hills,
their flanks and joints of rounded stone.
From time to weathered time she stops,
gneiss or granite socketing tired hips,
and gazes coastwards at the selvedge
of her images pared to grey. She builds

in planes and sinuosities, birch, root,
moss. Her art of meander gathers earth
layers flaked by the rust of thought,
horizons that break at jags of charcoal
pine, the blanks and missteps of the eye
let deep into her composition. Clefts
and pressure lines cool into pixels,
graphite washed in northern light set
aglow by our technology, the place
making content on the mineral page.

Growing Advice

At all costs avoid the twisted or winding pathway so often seen in the small garden situated on the corner where two streets meet.

— THE COMPLETE NEW ZEALAND GARDENER

You can make it work if you're at all
handy, hunkered and humble. It costs
only rain and the sun's incandescence (avoid
hatless noons) along with the twisted
complicity of leafy time unwinding.
Bump the wheelbarrow up the pathway,
tread, rake, tease and weed so often
peas will bloom as soon as you're seen in
flip-flops and crocuses flag your small
vernacular seasons because the garden
is making something of you, situated on
the border of dirt and thumb, the corner
with its stepover wall where two streets
grow neighbourly and flora and animal meet.

Blackcurrants

Sodden silver after rain, a tint to break
upon my tongue: all velvet ink and jangle
dropping wet like dew from the stem.

Come again, come again, cupped palm
and stalking fingers for the plump, syrupy
slip, the burgeoning give and skin-split.

Go in, laden, watch wax-eyes gleam
round the shoots, blackbirds hop and pluck
under the rattle of drying leaves.

Already an autumnal husk in that sound
though the fruit feels eternal, cell by link by
pearl to fill these stooping days.

Sunstrike

whited by afternoon haze
one car when the others brake
skims through the lights and bears
her with blind lip-biting momentum on
this middle-aged Phaeton reining the wheel
with her other hand shading as if to pat the sun
down where it belongs: fold your wings halcyon
with her other hand shading as if to stop the sun
reining the wheel for a lip-bitten moment
this middle-aged Phaeton borne blind
skims through the lights just beyond
one car when the others brake
whited by afternoon haze

Dark Skies

The air through which we look upon the stars,
is in a perpetual tremor.
　　　　　　　　— ISAAC NEWTON, *OPTICKS*

I raise my palm to blinker the streetlights'
dehydrated yellow and make out

what city after city covers: dark,
flung somewhat thin over these suburbs

yet welling up before me, stars,
like dropped stitches in the black,

their attenuated mica scatter
glinting in our fortunate night.

The air is less cluttered here, its tremor
and the moon's bright librations

ring nearly clear and the Milky Way
is a river we can travel to look

upon in regions reserved as parks.
Newton never strained his eye

against an oil-slick skyglow; a sleepless
dream unknown to astronomers

who lifted their lenses on hills
or towers towards the revolving skies.

Or dug concaves into the ground,
mouths that caught no slantwise rays

from the earth's blinding lustre
but threw upon their walls the lures

of glow-worm constellations:
grottoes of seasonless reflection,

philosophers' crypteria where 'the stars
might be observed even at noon'.

Once, when I asked a boy from Hong Kong
what new things he'd seen here,

he answered, 'the moon'.

Walking Is Controlled Falling

I have made a mistake.
Out in this aching stasis of frost
surfaces plane away from me
tiny down there, and an airlock has closed.

The shops feel distant as cold suns.
I am scared to go beyond my toes.
I watch their snub grips like a dentist
step, muffled step, up the brittle
spangled path the light forgot.

Day comes by degrees.
Cars crunch past through crevasses
scattering bones and every gravel sits
toothed in shadow.

Have I ventured so close to old?
I think of the slip of a sole
and my heart fuses.

Once the tyres slid. Just once.
A slight and gracious sidle
to the kerb. I sat, the wheel numb.
Said sorry to my mother who was
beside me in that momentary black
and now is gone.

I have moved south. It happens.
We orbit that icy continent
and brush against its loss.
The frost is precious and will lift.
I wrap myself and go on, walking and falling.
I may never get used to this.

Round Hill

Hill don't shrug, well short of the sky,
a strong shout from the nearest suburb.

I see you in the middle of the day,
dented like a mattress. Trudging sullen, winter brown.

Who has folded away your sheep?
Without them you are bare,
picking at the seams of your fencelines.

It's difficult to stand out, being Round Hill.
Snow rarely descends and wind musses you often.

Down the valley of pooling frost
trucks won't let you rest, squaring and backing, their ticking lights.

Someone must drive that track I pace by eye.
Someone else must keep vigil
over your scrubby shoulders.

Hill, take heart. I have seen you careful and pale
in low sun brushed with its pollen.

Mammoths

Time crumples in Duntroon, this afternoon
valley where, car-droned and signposted,
we walk among rockish tongues.

Above a flush of irrigated green
break those massy bergs, the tips of eras
thrusting into leaching light.

Like loaves, crumb soft to the touch,
the limestone pores and pits wherever
turf washes back. Yellow at first,

surprised into sun then growing grey
rind, layering down, comfortable
in the land's grazed lap.

Look, thrown on this paddock:
a herd of beast-headed
knucklebones, millennia-sized.

We climb and knead to feel how
these rocks dispose of gravity,
their shadow-play, the weather they make.

See them tumble, hide and seek
each other's grassy echoes, stone
people who clamber, laughing, for an hour

then drive away. While dusk infolds
the boulders and taniwha doze
with cetaceans' teeth in the deep.

Headland

That flat cliff abuts sea so hard
I feel it in my brow: steady
flinchless southward facing.

Like the gnomon of a sundial,
cleft by cast light
it alters without budging.

No getting around
its perseverance, how it juts
blunt into whetted white

undercut by water's wire
as the coastline bears,
strains against distance.

There, the full tide occurs:
what it is to carve
the moon's curve into the bays.

Walking that fretted wind-
bald hull lets me wave
at what planets know:

to bulk, cratered and doubting
spun through mist;
to lean out,
a blank buttress on a ledge of space.

On Kamau Taurua

The sun subsides, the island falls
away beneath the cliff path, twilight
wicking from tidal sands that run
dreaming and vast towards night's stars.

The people on the shore, tuned down,
move the black and compact
oystercatchers on, whose red cries
point the calm like the channel lights.

In the futile dusk, other calls haunt
across the water, extinguished voices
in the harakeke rustling with the sound
of nothing now but thistle and grass.

As if through pebbled glass the figures below
grey and dim, the seaborne current
draws out before them; underfoot,
history's silt and iron, its rocky cemeteries.

Miro

A tree came over me,
linchpin of the bush slope
where I stopped. Great swags
shook from its branches.

Like a container ship
offshore, its shade moved
across my sleep that night,
a long life's thought.

Waking with its trunk
growing through my brain;
for a moment's span
utterly ingrained.

The Beings

And then I saw them
speak up dark and choral:
a pair of yews, upstanding
in livery of whorled bristle and bow.

They had been living as I
passed through, as pillars
blinker paths beyond
wrought-iron gates.

Now those obelisks blazed
adamant green: one broader-beamed,
the other fissured with day.
Within their woody vaults

ancestral syllables coined
by a thousand reigns
of rust and verdigris
iuu, īwa, yw, grew strange.

Beyond recognition, the beings
who remain.

Willow

The willow won't grow tidily
not like the pin-tucked church
over the road its roots are doubtless
under-meshing, ditched in our runoff
drinking camber rain and feeling
for the pulse of my friend's steps
brushing through the grasses.
In her black coat she thinks a neat,
familiar shape into the farmland;
walking the bounds, looking after
this tree's steading. Wind-quakes
silver a canopy that twists up
skyward like a private storm
within this day's settled sun; such
sweet split memories in the torque
of that trunk, in the cast of her head,
in the red door and hearthsmoke
and the dented clover by the fence
where the willow watched me
press this spoor into the tangle,
a tired animal resting.

Prevailing

What can wear this wind
that weights the air?

Nothing moves but leans,
thrashes or bears stonewards.

Hills heel, the downbeat sea
stalling on its waves.

Eucalypts belly and flash,
torrents of pewter.

Only harriers hook on,
hang for the veer.

In the world one steady point:
the head of a hawk.

Shelter

Macrocarpas claw the sky,
they hiss and whip, splintered green explosions.
All my life I have never known
them sapling or tender. But old, old,
like the ghost tree whose gunmetal pillar
told the secret place at the heart of the bush
where we barefoot children met.

Those on this farm loom sombre in midsummer.
Serried into a stand, dense as a scrum
they chill the day, lend no shelter
for the sun. Wind heaves and their cold deepens.
They sweep an ancient unease into me, like the past
where it masses on the borders.

Staggering the other boundary: a row of stumps,
dead and rooted at the ankles as if sunk.
Even under rain their raw pale rounds look drained.
The nor-easter lashes in wet scrawled gusts,
recalling maybe where its voice once
branched and sang, before the chaw
before the crash, blank gaps blooming one by one,
a paddock thrumming. I grow a kind of sympathy
for the shelterbelt thrown.

As on another day, along a low-water strand,
I stumble on the hobbled line of a hedge
long cut down. This time undermined by sand,
a silver-black rictus of roots gripping nothing
but eroding tides. Like trenched sentries buried,
now exposed to a barer sun, this cankered air.

And again the wind courses in,
shakes the linked-arm shades of the trees
under whose echoes children will go,
and sheep lie down among scattered bark, defused cones.
Whether holding or giving way, they will never be young,
those wild, gnarled macrocarpas,
carried on the shoulders of their kin,
marching their dark detonations up the hills.

Murmurations

Black shaken sky, bird-sown
    dark grain over ploughed earth raining.

                        Flicker song of white between:
           hollows, hushes, rushing —
how many
        many
               cross-hatched myriads?

Starlings, falling over Europe.

            Black needles swing,
        steep drops,
mysterious lilts
       in the numbers.
            Thickets roll back,
        curl and fold,

        gone

           like smoke
                    from farms.

Trees hang winter wires, fencelines stark

and the fields

a dry riverbed.

Riroriro

We stopped on the track, pierced
by one plumb note that almost
compassed the forest. The dazzled
tangle of the trees awash with moss,
fern and cloudlight did not fall open
but now it held direction.
Something flickered with intent
there, there. Another bird, looping
in for the fuss and hopeful crunch
our bodies had made. We ceded
all motion, gathered to wait.
Meanwhile the track cut forward,
laboured and bootless. We stood
at an edge, under breath, no longer
any centre. All lines were casting
out above our heads: the peep, seek,
lure and flight of fledgling curiosity.
In webs of space between tree and
eye wove beings of feather, bone
so hollow they could slip right
through the twigs leaving behind
just their song. And where the riroriro
went or even if that was their call
is uncertain, only that we walked on.

Maelstrom

An outcry of terns electrifies a crag
clamouring of accident and stricken flesh

for what blows them onshore is both death
and occupation: life's great gyre

drawing them home to this rock,
this event that may take place any century

when terns storm in, cartwheeling
as if to keep the fuming air

ploughed by their wings, claiming
their quarter with metallic calls.

In the tapered chase, some birds dip,
quicksilver beaks flashing fish

to offer mates aground, folded
close in prayer that all will hold:

the nest scrape, the bob-dance, the pair
fronting the perishing wind —

generations on this outcrop over sand
near the chassis of a gull picked clean.

Penguin Colony, est. 1992

Blasted amphitheatre, disused quarry
glaring under the arc lights of day

like a neolithic dig; that drama
of ringed stone, post holes, littered bone

restaged inside this enceinte, strange-
scale, among birds. We clock

their emerging from earthworks,
concerted and pressed for time

and scaffold their paths because
they braid into ours long past, linking

water, sustenance, the nest. Of mounded
land let mouths shelter mothers

and with pens shut out the enemy,
stockade this model village

its red gables, boardwalks and grand-
stand ready for the encounter.

But no one tours today, the centre locked
against plague, residents burrowed

under the cape. At the ring fence
concrete-broken water mines away

our fortifications. In the silent stadium
swells clap like slamming doors.

(bird of unknown affinities)

the screen sieves up

        a bone

a lone nicotine yellow

        looks akin

stub of breast-keel

        but differs from

half a wishbone

        may belong

being all we hold of

        remains uncertain

Manu antiquus (old

        found near penguin

bird) who gives

        suggestive of albatross

this crone finger

        would-be pelican

to our sorting tables

        associated with

in order to roam

        incertae sedis

unbroken badlands

        (no place set)

with her relations

        yet

untold

Eye Contact

What heart must bellow in that bull.
The woman in the red coat stands

ten paces, steadies the lens.
Out of shot, sea lions hummock

on their haul-out. Cloaked in cooler sand,
they make the shoulder shapes of hills.

Whakahao rears to a cliff:
black ledge of sea-breasting chest,

disdainful nose. The photographer's
doubled eye blinks back.

The blue-dark offing steepens, refracts,
relaxes. The bull heaves, sniffs

towards his rival image. Then avalanches
into shallows, a wave briefly shadowed.

The Inlet's Shore

flat and prosey
— MARGINALIA IN A BOOK OF POEMS

Two chevroned feathers
from a paradise duck's breast
caught on knitted turf so smooth
they wafted into my fingers.

Their carpet was of water pimpernel
beside the glasswort groves
along the inlet's shore woven
with shells and mellow seagrass.

Flat, it was, manytoned drabs
of sand, gleam and sun-shot
emerald marching in low drones
to the dunes and distant hills.

Under a milky light, pied birds
went about stooped, gleaning
the speckled field; others hung
dark on the band of the sea.

In that wavering horizon,
where the merest snag loomed
I found a dull, sedate beauty,
an abundance of swans.

Yes, despite the red fire flush
tipping the succulent wort
and a stilt's elegant flight
the marsh was flat, almost poetry.

Knifefisher

Striker, on the brim
of water's singing bowl

you keep the future
locked in your raked

beak, for eternity holding
that turquoise sun,

a steady sentry
poised as a jeweller's scale.

This, the meniscus your dart
pierces — before

the perch
can flex, a foregone

decision in the fletch
of your tail

hooks a life clear,
dashed on the air-

thin edge of is
and gone, ripples floundering.

Albatross

When they fly, I soar
and laugh at my
heart stretched
high as expanse
will follow, pivoting
round a jet eye,
wing-line leading
that leisurely skim
resting on the curve
along the felt slip
of air speed, just so, just
adjusted to the lilt
of a pinion.

It's like
shaking out
a tent inside me,
fresh from bracing slopes
whenever my body pulls in, up,
into that air a bird makes
malleable as ocean water
and with presiding waver
over fractal land
forms flowing under
wing round again
sweeps the great
porcelain span of toroa
young and full of strut, clack
feather but above all forever flight
and the scent
of wind.

An Environmental History

The book hurts but I go on reading.
It doesn't take long once we come to it:
sharp as an adze blow, ash blaze, rats' teeth,
whalebone, deals done, a swift overrun.
The toll of knock-on consequences
like a ship's wake razing shore upon shore
is a line too often sung. Eaten, exhausted,
our stores of regret for the flightless dead.

Down on the beach, gulls are feeding.
All I do for today is watch each fend
their patch as terns zone in, heads cocked.
Fish shirr water, fleet away to their own resources.
Ponderous, as if evolving only now, dimly
feeling something has changed, chitons
graze the rock. There is food in books, too,
better knowing, but until we come to that
let algae, plankton, foliage flourish
long enough to keep the survivors fed.

Volcanic Harbour

All the way upon ashes,
foot upon soil, stone upon wall
with ghosts of boundary, hawthorn and byre,
I hack the fence's course towards the clouds.
In this roofless museum,
the air is clean enough for lichens
and other small, diversified ventures:
snaring weka or felling bush, churning butter,
industry clinging on where even bracken
takes a boulder for shelter.
Higher into the cooled-sweat wind
the stream-murmur lapses.
Hard to call back ferns or forested steeps
from this mangy, heat-worn grass,
hear kākāpō boom across gullies
of magpies, gums and cracking macrocarpa;
hard to taste the fat of this land showing bone,
falling away on every side.
The pull of space opens wings
while my grasp holds footing by the claims
of yellow catsear, marker poles;
thistle flowers, fat and heraldic,
a stag's head in a scoured log.
Straddling the summit, the trig bangs its drum:
all this way but never the first.
In the future forest, saplings
near the streambed volunteer signs
of green. Once more sky cloaks the cone
and from the molten sea the view scuds over,
blotting and amnesiac. A raw mist closes in
this broken arbour of coprosma,
this linked ring of combusted rock.
I sit on a stone and let time work.

Prospect of Refuge

Walking all day could harbour us here,
under this quelled sun, how it leans down
to diminish the trees and let the ever-present
sound lap the bays, the brushstrokes of salt water.
There's an unruliness in this calm, the ragged
intrusions of branches pared by gales, notches
subsiding in eroded clay. Headlands are clinker-
built boats upturned, tarpaulined for shelter.
Meanwhile the blush, the discretion of distance,
what was said, what should have been, tidings
of pebbles, shell shards, wrack. They come in
with us, unwelcomed, carried into the coves.
What else we might say is of that same strain:
the settled sea, love, a brief abatement.

Between Together and Alone

The hut is for one, so she shows me down,
grass swishing round my gumboots, damp
seeping through the splits at the heels. I lever
them off inside the door while the hut unpacks its walls
and sets up the folding chair, its plywood light.
For a long time after she has left I am struck
within the frame of that dumb, pot-watching suspense.
It's important not to move to see what moves.
The numb pinch of cold. The webs, the wet.
One pīwakawaka: shuttlecock across glass.

I have been up at the house, near people, unable.
Woodstove warmth lingers in my clothes,
women's herbal voices, but sometimes among villages
I am sitting a beat apart, holding a box.
Squarely shut, it must not be shaken nor overturned.
The box is the shape of this hut, where I carry it
to rest cross-legged on the chest pulled up to the window.

Soft rain. Across the gully, sopping bush, dripping
creeper and lichen. The sun stares back at me
through rice-water clouds delicate as the skin
between together and alone. My body folds
limbs and ribs around the box, fumbles in, finds
an empty bowl. Made by hands, perhaps
by those friends, to catch the conversations
swilling round this place in roots, trickles, calls.
A pair of pīwakawaka, then more: droplets flicked
from the fencewire. They draw me out, scribbling this
way then that. They look like they're chasing air
but I have to believe in the tea-scoops of nourishment there.

On my walk back up I pretend with the fantails,
chirrup and whistle to their chiding squeaks
as if we're all good with people
instead of liking to be around them only at times
for petty hungers or awkward flutters; too near or not
nearly close to the unseen between one another.
Over the hill lies the rain-mazed sea, that oldest means
of communication, circling like thumb and forefinger
the lonely latitudes. To the village
I carry the hut and the pīwakawaka, who fly off,
and the box of quiet and the open-handed bowl.

Tairua

mostly it's the river
handy and tannin sweet
playing with rocks

and if a tangled kid
pads down in shorts
to skim a stone

just a flicker paws
mānuka-printed water
where she's gone

Notes

'Verona by the Leith' was written after a Dunedin Summer Shakespeare performance of *Romeo and Juliet* directed by Kim Morgan in Woodhaugh Gardens on 31 January 2020.

'On Hume's Table' quotes from David Hume's *An Enquiry Concerning Human Understanding* (1748) in stanza 1, and *A Treatise of Human Nature* (1739) in stanza 2. Rousseau's comment is reproduced in Thomas Edward Ritchie, *An Account of the Life and Writings of David Hume* (1807).

'Dark Skies': 'the stars might be observed even at noon' (spelling modernised) and the description of crypteria are from Henry Wotton, *Elements of Architecture* (1624).

'The Artist's Site' was inspired by the website and artworks of Chrys Allen at www.chrysallen.co.uk.

'(bird of unknown affinities)' takes its title and adapts some phrases from an entry on New Zealand Birds Online.

'Blue-tide' and 'Prospect of Refuge' were written for the collaborative project *CUMULUS: An Anthology of Skies* (Caselberg Press, 2023) in response to the photography of Carlos Biggemann.

Acknowledgements

Thanks are due to the editors of the publications where some poems have previously appeared: *Landfall, Otago Daily Times, Poetry New Zealand* and *takahē*. I am grateful to the Caselberg Trust for awarding me the Elizabeth Brooke-Carr Emerging Writers Residency at Broad Bay, where several of these poems were written. For their encouragement and critique, my warmest thanks go to the members of the Blacks Road Poetry Workshop. I would like to thank Anna Hodge, Claire Lacey, Carolyn McCurdie and the anonymous readers for their feedback on the manuscript, and Sue Wootton, Fiona Moffat, Meg Hamilton and Mel Stevens at Otago University Press for their support. Many writing friends offered advice and hospitality, among them Majella Cullinane, Lynley Edmeades, Kirstie McKinnon, Lissa Moore, Emma Neale, Louise Wallace and Sophia Wilson. Special thanks go to my brother, John Kitching, for the cover photograph.

Published by Otago University Press
533 Castle Street
Dunedin, New Zealand
university.press@otago.ac.nz
www.oup.nz

First published 2023
Copyright © Megan Kitching
The moral rights of the author have been asserted

ISBN 978-1-99-004856-2

Published with the assistance of Creative New Zealand

Editor: Anna Hodge
Design: Fiona Moffat

Cover photograph: John Kitching

Printed in New Zealand by Ligare.